# What's it like to be a...
# FARMER

Written by Morgan Matthews
Illustrated by Anne Kennedy

**Troll Associates**

**Special Consultant:** Vincent Poloniak
*Member of the New York State Farm Bureau;*
*Man of the Year Award, Agricultural Stabilization and*
*Conservation Committee—Department of Agriculture.*

*Library of Congress Cataloging-in-Publication Data*

Matthews, Morgan.
    What's it like to be a farmer / by Morgan Matthews; illustrated
by Anne Kennedy.
        p.    cm.—(Young careers)
    Summary: Follows a farmer and his family through the year as they
raise crops and animals.
    ISBN 0-8167-1803-2 (lib. bdg.)     ISBN 0-8167-1804-0 (pbk.)
    1. Farmers—Juvenile literature.  2. Farm life—Juvenile
literature.  3. Agriculture—Vocational guidance—Juvenile
literature.  [1. Farmers.  2. Occupations.]  I. Kennedy, Anne,
1955-    , ill.  II. Title.  III. Series.
S519.M27  1990
630′.2′03—dc20               89-34386

# What's it like to be a...
# FARMER

Plowed Fields

Silo

Shed

Barn

Vegetable
Garden

Farmhouse

It's springtime at Smith Farm. What a busy
time! The whole family is up early. There's
much to do—and everyone helps!

The Smith family likes running a farm. They know farming is a very important job. Farmers grow most of the food we eat. Mr. Smith knows how to grow plants. He knows about soil, weather, and animals. Some farmers learn these things in school. Others, like Mr. Smith, learn by growing up on farms.

Some farmers grow only one kind of crop, like corn. Others raise only one kind of animal, like chickens. A mixed farm, like the Smith Farm, raises many crops and animals.

Farmers do different jobs at different times of
the year. Why is spring such a busy time at
Smith Farm? Spring is planting time.
"Let's get busy," says Mr. Smith.

*Shed*

*Vegetable
Garden*

The children run out of the farmhouse. Smith
Farm has many buildings. There is a big barn
and a tall silo, for storing corn. There are pens
for animals and sheds for machinery.

Jenny runs to the barn.

"I'll feed the chickens," she calls.

Little Tommy answers, "I'll get water for the pigs."

The children do many jobs around the farm before they leave for school.

Mrs. Smith goes to the big vegetable garden.
There's weeding to do. Many vegetable plants
fill the garden. When summer comes, there will
be plenty of tomatoes, peppers, and carrots.

Mr. Smith goes to a shed. He gets on a tractor. Tractors help the farmer do many jobs. They make the hard work a lot easier.

Mr. Smith drives the tractor to a big field. Farms have many wide, open fields where crops are planted. Mr. Smith wants to plant wheat in this field.

Tractor

Shed

The field's soil has been made rich with manure. Rich soil helps the seeds to quickly grow into strong plants. But before the seeds are planted, the soil must be dug up. That is called plowing.

*Moldboard Plow*

A plow is added to the tractor. Up and down the field goes Mr. Smith. Big chunks of dirt are dug up. The field is plowed in neat rows.

Mr. Smith cannot plow all the fields by himself. In another field, Mrs. Smith also uses a tractor. During busy times, the Smiths hire other helpers, too. After days of work, the plowing is done.

Disk Harrow

Seeds cannot grow in big chunks of dirt. The fields must be made flat and smooth. Mr. Smith adds a harrow to his tractor. The disk harrow breaks the chunks of dirt into tiny pieces.

15

Jenny and Tommy are working, too. Jenny is putting sheep out to pasture. There are many baby sheep, or lambs. Lambs are born in the spring.

"Lambs are funny," Jenny says, as she watches them jump and play.

In the barn Tommy is feeding his horse. Long ago, farm horses did the work of tractors. This horse is Tommy's pet.

In the fields Mr. Smith is ready to sow, or plant, seeds. A planting machine is on the tractor.

Wheat is planted in neat rows. *Plunk! Plunk! Plunk!* In go the seeds.

Seed Drill

Seed Drill

Mrs. Smith is planting corn. Different crops
are raised in different fields.

To grow, seeds need sun, water, and rich soil. Up sprout the seeds. They grow and grow. By summer, the seeds have grown into plants.

Summer brings new work. It is time to make hay. The hay will be eaten by the farm animals during the cold winter months. Fields of grass are cut. The grass is put in rows. The hot sun dries the grass into hay.

Hay

Mower

*Bales*

*Baler*

A hay baler goes on the tractor. It scoops up loose hay. *Whoosh!* Out it comes in a large bundle called a bale. Bales of hay are tossed into a wagon.

They take the hay to the barn. Up go the bales on a conveyor belt. The hay is stored in the barn. Now the farm animals will have enough to eat.

Barn

Conveyor
Belt

Wagon

Fields of green corn have been cut. Every bit of the corn plant has been chopped up. A machine blows it into the tall silo for storage. Later animals will eat the corn.

*Silo*

The summer sun shines. It ripens the garden vegetables. The Smiths have a roadside stand. People stop to buy the beautiful, fresh vegetables.

"The tomatoes look nice," says a customer. "I'll take a basket of them."

Combine

Wheat

Soon it is fall—the busiest time of all. Crops must be harvested before bad weather ruins them. The Smiths hire helpers to cut the wheat.

*Combine*

A special machine cuts wheat. It is a combine. *Whoosh! Whoosh!* The combine cuts down wheat stalks and collects the grain.

After the wheat is harvested, cut-up stalks called straw are left behind in rows. Later the straw can be baled. After much work all of the crops are harvested.

Straw

Mr. Smith then sells his crops. The wheat
becomes flour for bread. The Smiths make
money by selling crops, vegetables, and animals.

Winter comes. It's time to repair machinery. Tommy helps fix the tractor. Animals are cared for. Mrs. Smith and Jenny feed chopped corn to the cattle.

Winter is also a time for planning.
"Next spring, let's plant corn in that field."
Mr. and Mrs. Smith agree.

A snowy farm is a great place to play.

Would you like to be a farmer?